SEGOVIA
in your hand

editorial **en su mano**

First Edition April 1984
Ediciones En Su Mano
(«In Your Hand» Editions)
C/ Ferraz, 34. Madrid
Tel. 433 82 99
Photographs: M. Corral, Carlos Miguel Jr. and
those furnished by the Secretary of State for
Tourism
Graphic Design by: Florencio García
Written by: J. M. Fernández Gaytan
Technical Advisor: Pablo M. Valdés
Historical Advisor: Julio Cilleros
I.S.B.N.: 84-86320-02-X
D.L.: M. 17321-1984
Printed by Egraf, S. A.
Polígono Industrial de Vallecas
C/G, s/n. Madrid-31
Printed in Spain
typesetting: COE, S. A.
Translated by Muriel Feiner

Prologue

Segovia has been, is and always will be an endless source of inspiration for writers, poets, painters, historians, archaeologists and every lover of the Fine Arts and beautiful things. Because Segovia is above all else beautiful and majestic for those of us who live here and for those who come to visit. In fact, it would be very rare indeed for someone to get to know Segovia and not fall victim to her charms. Many of the people who have fallen into her «trap» were victims of a kind of mermaid's song, like that which seduced Ulysses and as they were not able to undo her spell, they have either moved here permanently or come to spend a week-end or a week, time and again.

In order to get to know Segovia and love her, in order to saturate oneself with the city, its spirit, its bewitchery, its tranquility and its gaiety, all you have to do is wander along the streets and squares, along the narrow alleyways, before the huge, majestic monuments and through the dreamy, bucolic outskirts of the city, and through its «green belt», dotted with monasteries, tree-lined boulevards, pine groves, wheat fields... Segovia is easy to visit because it is small and compact; you can almost fit it into the palm of your hand.

For this reason, «SEGOVIA IN YOUR HAND» turns out to be a charming book with a great deal of motivations. It does not give the impression of sufficiency, nor does it pretend to give lessons without being a titled professor. It merely intends to help the first-time visitor to appreciate the city's charms and if the reader visits Segovia with this book in his hand, he will learn to love the city as those of us who know it well love it. We would say that this book, dear reader, which you have in your hands, is more than just a guide book to the local art and monuments, it is a breath of inspiration to help you reach the true spirit of the city and discover the authentic charm of its simple yet busy life. Segovia, with the appearance of a pretty, demure young girl, nurtures a lively spirit, a quality of which not many cities can boast.

The authors of «SEGOVIA IN YOUR HAND» respect the inevitable obligation of informing the reader of the monumental, artistic and scenic attractions of the city and they have done this with brief but expressive descriptions and with the most necessary details. They have used the tempered pen of the true Castilian spirit, but with an informal style which helps us to get the feeling behind what the visitor is seeing with his own eyes.

The art, history, fine cooking and all of the other features which have made Segovia an unforgettable city are covered in literary description, which at times resorts to the aid of noted writers and poets, who have known and loved the city and have dedicated the best of their wits and pens to extoll her virtues. The book would not be complete without its projection to the rest of the province, whose geography encases an artistic sampling of castles, churches, palaces, mansions, gardens and tree-lined boulevards, with groves of unperishable green pines.

We can repeat that the whole literary work is at the same time concise yet rich in content, sincerity and emotion. It is complemented by a rosary of truly exemplary images, a photographic reflection of the immense charm which is found in this province, whose capital, Segovia, is an «irreplaceable crossroads for every historical roadway». And so, dear reader, we leave you with «SEGOVIA IN YOUR HAND».

PABLO MARTIN CANTALEJO
Director of the daily newspaper
«El Adelantado de Segovia»

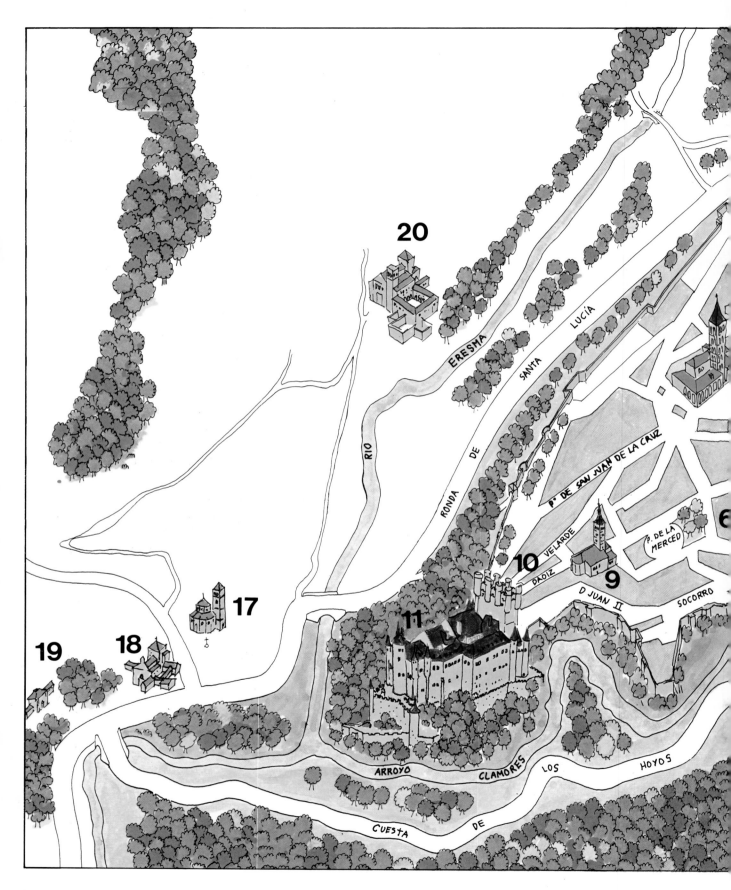

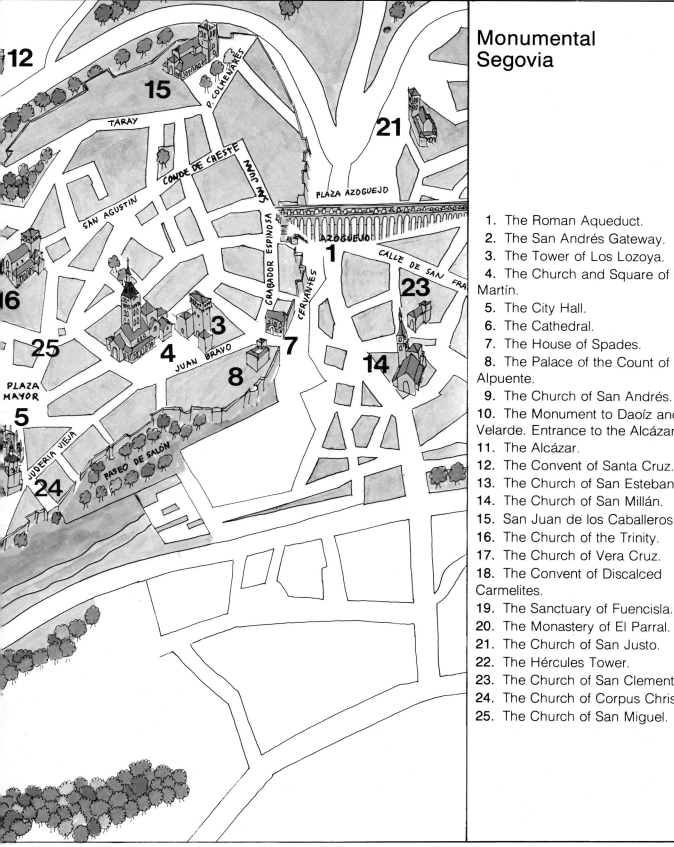

Monumental Segovia

1. The Roman Aqueduct.
2. The San Andrés Gateway.
3. The Tower of Los Lozoya.
4. The Church and Square of San Martín.
5. The City Hall.
6. The Cathedral.
7. The House of Spades.
8. The Palace of the Count of Alpuente.
9. The Church of San Andrés.
10. The Monument to Daoíz and Velarde. Entrance to the Alcázar.
11. The Alcázar.
12. The Convent of Santa Cruz.
13. The Church of San Esteban.
14. The Church of San Millán.
15. San Juan de los Caballeros.
16. The Church of the Trinity.
17. The Church of Vera Cruz.
18. The Convent of Discalced Carmelites.
19. The Sanctuary of Fuencisla.
20. The Monastery of El Parral.
21. The Church of San Justo.
22. The Hércules Tower.
23. The Church of San Clemente.
24. The Church of Corpus Christi.
25. The Church of San Miguel.

Index

Segovia, the capital

The surroundings/ The Castle Route

⬅ The Aqueduct.

The Aqueduct

We will classify the Aqueduct later on as Segovia's visiting card for this is in fact the case, though it is indeed much, much more. It is the very heart of the city because until you pass beneath its arches, you cannot really say that you are in Segovia. Just as Ramón Gómez de la Serna called it «the belltower for all the bells of the world», it has also been considered the coat of arms of the city, «yesterday's gold on a field of red, today, silver on Azure». And, for Jaime Delgado, «a pillar of air from which its miracle or artifice is suspended/from the divine vault of the heavens».

Over the Plaza del Azoguejo —«zoquejo», meaning small «Zoco» or Arab market place— the Aqueduct offers the waters of the Acebada river to the city. It appears that the Aqueduct was built between

the first and second centuries A. D. by Vespasian and Trajan. To give some figures, we can say that its maximum height is 28.29 meters and its length is 728 meters. It is made up of a total of 167 arches, which are arranged thusly: 75 simple arches which run from the San Ildefonso highway to the Díaz Sanz Square.

Al-Mamun of Toledo demolished a part of the Aqueduct in 1072 and the Catholic Monarchs, Ferdinand and Isabel, ordered its reconstruction in the 15th century, with thirty-six arches of Ogival curves. This was the only restoration work carried out on the structure until the very recent reinforcement of the pillars which support the endless traffic which develops around the Aqueduct.

But for what kind of city or population was a construction of this magnitude, with such a perfect combination of art and technology, designed? It is the pride of all humanity. The arrangement of its stones is like one huge puzzle, which has been solved to perfection. And it is not without its legend either. In

this case, the story relates that the water girl was very tired of filling her pitcher and carrying it back to her house on her hip. So, she offered her soul to the devil if he would only change the course of the waters to pass from one side of the low valley to the other, by means of a special structure which he would have to build over night. However, the girl suddenly repented and prayed to the Virgin for help. The rooster crowed before dawn: Just one stone was missing to complete the structure but it was enough for the devil to lose his bet and the girl saved her soul. Today, Segovia proudly displays in its coat of arms, one of the most important works every carried out in the history of mankind, and it does not really matter who was its true creator.

⊡ The Aqueduct, an aerial view.
⊟ A close-up view of the Aqueduct.
⊟ The San Andrés gateway.

The Gateways

Segovia is a city embraced in stone by the old ramparts which are kept in good condition. The city walls are hidden at some points by different buildings which were built directly into the walls to form a historical spinal column. However, for the most part, Segovia's walls can be appreciated with all their graceful plenitude and unique grandeur.

Segovia's walls should be attributed to the 11th and 12th centuries and its two and a half kilometer perimeter encases the upper part of the town. Despite its historical date and even its incrustations and later constructions, stone tablets have been found within the wall which remind us of Sextus

Severus, Publius Juvenal Juvenalis and other Roman names of even earlier times.

Only three of the original seven gateways are found in the wall today and of the doors which once existed, only one, which was reconstructed in 1947, can be used and two other doors have since been walled up.

The Gateways of San Andrés, Santiago and San Cebrián have been kept intact while those of Sol (The Sun), Luna (The Moon), San Juan and San Martín have been demolished. The San Martín Gateway rested against the so-called Casa de los Picos (House of Spades) which is perhaps the most famous home in Spain and it is certainly the most photographed.

The Puerta de San Andrés is in the best condition, with imposing

military design. It is supported by two sturdy towers; the one on the inside is square and the one on the outside is polygonal. It opens up onto the Clamores stream and it served as the customary entrance to the old Jewish quarter. There is a niche at the top, on the inside, which is dedicated to the Virgen del Socorro and in another place, there is a stone tablet which reminds the traveller of Quevedo's shrewd

opportunist, Don Pablos. The Gateway was restored in the times of Emperor Carlos I and again on a much more recent date by the Dirección General de Bellas Artes (General Board for the Fine Arts).

The other two gateways· which are kept in good condition open onto the Eresma Valley. The Santiago Gateway conserves the wall on one side but has lost it on the other due to a relatively recent landslide. It has a bold structure of a Mudejar style and is decorated with horseshoe arches which give it a hearty personality. The San Cebrián Gateway in the old section of the wall provides a unique intimate frame for an old sixteenth century stone cross.

⬆ The Santiago gateway.
↘ The San Cebrián gateway.
➡ The Santiago gateway.

⬆   The Tower of Los Lozoya. San Martín Square.

⬅☐   A house in the Merced (Mercy) Square.

⬅   The Secretary's House. Valdeláguila Street.

➡   The Aqueduct. A panoramic view.

The city

Every city in the world can offer us some specific attraction which will be enough to justify our visit. However, a prodigious effect is produced when we come to a place like Segovia where every little street, every square, every building, every stone define by themselves a page of history, a monument, a captivating landscape, a legend or a miracle.

Such is the traveller's sensation upon his first or twenty-first visit to this city of Saints and Kings, nobles and revolutionaries, incredible architects both known and unknown, hearty men of arms and hopeless dreamers. A combination of all of the above and much, much more is «Segovia, the Victorious», according to its old Celtic translation. It has more than two millenniums of existence on its shoulders and is secure in its legitimate pride and creative spirit.

As an echo and consequence of the above, it does not seem really wise to recommend one or more specific itineraries for our journey. If the traveller has enough time and if he so wishes, he would do better in granting full freedom to his feet, to allow them to select their own course at random. He should climb, descend, advance, retreat, stop and admire at his own rate, the one thousand and one surprises which he will come across continuously, whatever the route he has so capriciously chosen. Because

Segovia is a unique world for the visitor, as evidenced by its calling card, the Aqueduct, which has celebrated its two thousandth anniversary in 1974.

As if it were floating on an infinite sea of plains which marks its outline, Segovia has sailed through centuries of history with the special bearing and dignity of its people and its works. Its dozens of towers appear as tall masts ready to hoist sails every day against the winds which have always driven it forward in a sea-going fashion and which many illustrious pens have comprehended from the image of the sturdy prow of the brave Alcazar Castle.

The visitor can never go straight ahead through its streets. To the contrary, he will feel obliged to stop at every corner, in every doorway, at the foot of every tower, at every typical Segovian engraved tiling which is an incomparable art which enhances and adorns so many of the city's buildings.

As Vicente Marrero said in his pure, fraternal verse: «In the truth of the plain/everything is covered with gold, Segovia on high/cleanly rises up». And we can all go with her, as if taken by her hand, with the constant memory of her history which is deeply rooted in the trail of Hercules the Egyptian. Traces of Hercules were identified by many in Santo Domingo el Real, in the Tower of Hercules, in the Iberian sculpture of «urbis conditor», which treads upon the head of an enormous wild boar, an image which appears on the cover of «History of Segovia», by Diego de Colmenares in his first edition, dated in the year 1640.

Its Roman origins are culminated in the medieval, 12th and 13th centuries with its very beautiful Romanesque churches, around which the town grew up. It was rich in every type of craftsman and there were more than fifty different specialties, even in the year 1570. The decadence which followed the War of the Communities was replaced in the present century by a new and stimulating horizon, inspired by Tourism, which makes it possible for us to look forward to a promising, bright future.

The facades of the mansions of San Martín Square.

The City Hall.

⬆ Arias Dávila tower.
⬅☐ Typical Segovian engraved tiling.
⬅ The Juan Bravo Theatre.

The Cathedral

She has been called the «Great Lady of Cathedrals» and rightfully so, due to the grace and presence of its 88 meter high tower. The original Cathedral, together with the Alcazar, consecrated in 1228, was almost entirely destroyed during the War of the Communities. Later, by order of Emperor Carlos I, construction on the new Cathedral was undertaken in the year 1525.

The highest point in the city was selected for its construction but it was necessary to first demolish a hundred homes and the old Convent of the nuns of St. Clare. This construction was one of the last works of late Gothic style to be built in Spain despite the fact that at that time the Renaissance style was imposing itself in our country. It is 105 meters long, 50 meters wide and the height of its central nave is 33 meters.

Juan Gil de Hontañón, the Master of the new Cathedral of

Salamanca, directed the first phase of the work until his death, upon which he was succeeded by his son Rodrigo, who was aided by García de Cubillas, the quantity surveyor of the first architect. Other names to be mentioned, though they intervened much later were Juan de Mugaguren, responsible for the dome above the transept in 1620, which replaced the tall spire destroyed by a bolt of lightning in 1614; and Pedro de Brizuela, from Segovia, who at the beginning of that same century built the northern facade of San Frutos in Herrerian style. Of special interest in this wall is the niche which shows us the Patron Saint of the Diocese carved in stone. Francisco Vázquez and Alonso Martínez also took part in this enormous work.

Consecrated in 1768, its large windows, gargoyles and flying buttresses lure the visitor from the outside, and together they make up one of the most impressive Cathedrals in the whole country. The Puerta del Perdón (Doorway of Forgiveness) opens at the foot of the temple and a stone image of the Immaculate Conception appears in it. In the southern arm of the transept we find the door dedicated to Segovia's first bishop, San Geroteo.

But at this point, before visiting the interior of this magnificent Cathedral, we should consider an event which might seem trivial after all these years but in truth, it accurately reflects the enthusiastic and generous feelings of the entire Segovian townsfolk. When the time came, the entire town took part in the first phases of the Cathedral's construction, with contributions, the offering of building material and even with their personal efforts and labor, if that was all their capital.

↑ The Cathedral. An aerial view.
← The Cathedral as seen from the Clamores stream.
→ The rear facade of the Cathedral.

The inside of the Cathedral of Santa María is simply grandiose; there is no other word for it. It was built in the shape of a Latin cross and the three naves which make it up are separated by circular pillars. There is a total of seven absidal chapels.

Commissioned by Carlos III, Sabatini himself took charge of the construction of the Main Altar, using marble, jasper and gilded bronze, with the help of silversmith Antonio Vendetti. The Gothic image of Our Lady of Peace is venerated here and some say it was offered by King Fernando III el Santo (the Saint) and according to others, by King Enrique IV.

The visitor will surely stop to contemplate the choir stalls which came from the old temple. They were carved in the second half of

the fifteenth century and were a donation from Bishop Juan de Arias Dávila.

If we enter through the San Frutos doorway, to the right, we see the Chapel of La Piedad (Pity), with an altarpiece by Juan de Juni, dated in 1571. The triptych of the Descent from the Cross is a masterpiece by the Flemish artist Ambrosio Benson. Then, the Chapel of San Cosme and San Damián, with the «Immaculate

Conception» by Gregorio Fernández. Next is the Chapel of the Conception which houses quite valuable paintings, some of which are by Ries. The chapel also has a splendid mahogany grille work.

Opposite this chapel, we find the one with the «Recumbent Christ» by Gregorio Fernández; that of Santa Bárbara, with the baptism font donated by Enrique IV; and the Chapel of Santiago, with a painting by Segovian artist Alonso de Herrera, which was at one time attributed to Pantoja de la Cruz. And finally, the Chapel of the Sagrario (Tabernacle), with its ceramic altar by Daniel Zuloaga and a Christ by Pereira.

Works attributed to Berruguete, Morales, Van Eyck and Benvenuto Cellini, among others, can be visited in the Cathedral's museum, where

one can also see interesting sculptures including the Recumbent Tomb of Pedro de Castilla, the infant prince who fell from a window in the Alcázar to his death in 1366. And, of course, the magnificent processional monstrance, the work of silversmith Rafael González. It was presented in the Corpus Christi day processions of 1656. We should also make mention of the fifteenth century Gothic chalice, which was a

donation from Beltrán de la Cueva, and the silver altar which is made from six candelabras and three silver sacrum, all of which were donated by Bishop Martínez Escalzo.

Again, special mention is deserved by the Cathedral Archives which house a treasure of five hundred incunabla, an amount which can only be surpassed in Spain by the National Library and the Library of El Escorial. One of the most outstanding works found here is the «Synodal of Aguilafuente», dated 1472, which was one of the first books to be printed in Spain and some consider it to be indeed the very first.

We cannot forget the Chapter House with its collection of tapestries narrating the story of Zenobia, Queen of Palmira; nor any one of the remaining chapels, the Neo-classic retrochoir where the silver chest containing the bones of San Frutos is venerated; and the stained glass windows made in the middle of the sixteenth century by Flemish, Toledo-born and Salamancan craftsmen. They depict different subjects relating to the «Redemption of Christ».

And we cannot naturally pass by the Gobelin tapestries, the paintings by Valdés Leal and Esquivel, the coffered ceiling of the Chapter House itself, the magnificent carriage used to carry the Monstrance in the Corpus Christi processions, the noted Lectern kept in the Choir, the pulpit and the grille work located before the main altar, and, built into the Cloister wall in the rear, the tomb of María del Salto, the Jewess who gave birth to one of

◰ The inside tympanum. Cathedral.
◲ The Cathedral Cloister.
▸ The Cathedral. The choir stalls.

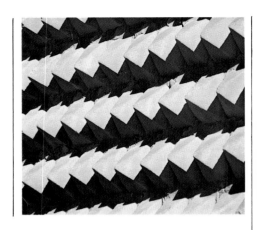

◢   A close-up view of the House of Spades.

◄►   San Martín Square. A fountain.

►   The House of the Count of Corres. San Martín square.

□►   The House of Spades. Facade.

the most beautiful legends of Segovia. We will relate her story a little later on.

In very few monuments can the visitor find such a haven of peace, a pleasure similar to the contemplation of the sum total of all of the art collected here over the years. Its fascinating monumental nature, on the other hand, shelters the endless rosary of buildings which make up and define this part of the town, as a mother hen protects her baby chicks.

What was an «enormous, mystical steamer» to José Ortega y Gasset, manages to always cover new runs in its uncontrollable navigation and its tireless binnacle. And if we have dared to outline a possible route to follow on the inside of the building, it has been done merely to give our readers a brief idea of what they may find. The ideal would surely be for the visitor to trace his own course, choose his own rate of walking and select each visit according to his own tastes and interests, with the recommendations furnished by a guide or book or simply guided by his own personal discoveries.

Because its walls, its stones, its works of art, give us an unmatched repertoire of the Cathedral's history, which began on June 8, 1525 when the cornerstone was set in place, we should take special note of the following: the star-studded, ribbed vaults; the images of San Frutos and San Geroteo, the main Patron Saint of the Diocese and the city's first bishop, respectively, the work of Manuel Adeba Pacheco (they are located in the Main Altar); the study of the manuscript which gives the most thorough details on the subject of stained glass windows and which is kept among the other very valuable manuscripts in the Cathedral's Archives; and the hundreds of miracles and treasures which would make this superficial list endless.

We find a sucession of naves, domes, facades, columns, pinnacles, mullions and one thousand details more that guard and treasure an authentic historical and artistic prodigy, so that whatever one's interest and preferences, his visit to the Cathedral will prove gratifying.

⬆ Monstrance carriage.
➡ San Justo.

The House of the Spades

It is one of the most well known and photographed buildings in the world, intended at the time of its construction to be the School of Arts and Crafts. Located in Juan Bravo street, it was constructed during the last third of the fifteenth century. It owes its popular name to the fact that each granite ashlar of the facade was finished off with a diamond point, under one of which, according to the legend, a fabulous treasure has been hidden.

But there is also another legend concerning this dwelling, which stood on a property belonging to the La Hoz family. It seems they were descendants of a religious convert and so the house was at one point known as the «House of the Jew». Francisco Ignacio de Cáceres explained that people continued to call the house thusly despite the family coat of arms which presided the keystone of its half-point facade and each balcony. Its owner created such an original geometric decoration which did very soon replace its previous, unappreciated nickname.

Talavera tiles decorate the hall and patio. The San Martín Gateway adjoined one end of the facade but a very regrettable municipal decision was responsible for its disappearance in 1883.

⬆   Church of San Andrés.

◨☐   The towers of San Esteban and San Andrés.

◨   The Church of San Justo; to the right, El Salvador.

The Alcázar Castle

Here, more than in any other place, the sea-faring vocation which we notice on every corner, takes greater form. José García Nieto tells us that «the poplars ascend from Segovia/to the seaworthy prow». In the powerful verse of Jaime Delgado, «the castle prow rents through the clouds/heavens reveal their wise custom/and tired of old astronomy/dead princes, courts, kings, ladies/sacrifice their secret artillery/and return to the dominions of the fates/the architectonic dream of the Alcázar/keeps vigil, sleeps, creates and lives». And José Luis Pernas, from another point of view, defines the sea, «I do not know how to explain it» and he chooses to say «it is simply immense/like all of your lands».

It is the confluence of the Eresma and the Clamores rivers, the spur which cuts the silence of the plain, a permanent, Castilian watchtower

which fulfills its mission of watching the passage of the centuries with impassive serenity. Everything seems to indicate that another fortress stood here during the Roman epoch and it was used as well by the Arabs.

After the reconquest of the city by Alfonso VI, the ancient manuscripts also refer to the Alcázar in the 12th century. Together with the Aqueduct and the Cathedral, the Alcázar, without a doubt, confers its authentic profile on the city of Segovia. After that initial period, it underwent further construction, expansions, restorations and additions.

From its Cistercian-Gothic style and from Alfonso el Sabio (The Wise), the Alcázar would receive the Court of the Sovereigns of Castile on different occasions, including Alfonso XI and Pedro the Cruel and the latter's conqueror, Enrique de Trastamara. This dynasty was determined, in the opinion of the Marquis of Lozoya, to convert the Alcázar «in the rival of the Andalusian Alcazares».

The Court was held there on different occasions and Isabel la Católica departed from the Alcázar in order to be crowned at the atrium of San Miguel as Queen of Castile. Felipe II married Ana of Austria there as well and, in addition, many famous people were imprisoned in the castle, such as the Duke of Medinaceli and the Duke of Guisa. Carlos III set up the Artillery College here and later the General Military Archives was also installed.

The visitor, with his sight set on its pointed, slate towers, comes close to the monument to Daoiz and Velarde (who were cadets here in the first Spanish Military Academy), the work of Segovian Marinas. The visitor then crosses the stone bridge which replaced the old wooden drawbridge which existed in the times of Felipe II and faces with unconcealable surprise the one hundred meter high Tower of Juan II, reticulated with the typical Segovian engravings.

The route which we will follow on the inside will take us across the Herrerian Patio of Arms or Honor Patio, in order to enter the Room of the «Ajimeces», containing different royal portraits, which are signed by Maffei, Casado del Alisal and Moreno Carbonero, and other historical scenes by José Madrazo and Salvador Viniegra. Two suits of armor complete the presentation of this room which receives its name precisely from its four interior

↘ The Alcázar castle as seen from the confluence of the Eresma and Clamores rivers.
↩ The Alcázar castle. Mosaic work.

↑ The monument to Daoiz and Velarde, in front of the Alcázar.

←□ The Juan II Tower.

← The entrance to the Alcázar.

windows. The visitor can appreciate the true meaning of this authentic Segovian watchman and can relive history in its paintings, which reflect some exceptional pages from our past.

In the Throne Room the platform of the Catholic Monarchs has been reconstructed with their coats of arms. It was the first room to be restored since 1940 and the Moorish frieze of gypsum kiln was completed. A coffered ceiling of

Mudejar interlacing arches taken from the Valladolid town of Urones de Castroponce was also added to replace the one which was lost in the fire of 1862.

At that time, the ceiling of the Galley Room was also lost. The room was called thusly because it was reminiscent of the hull of a ship. It was the next section to be restored and it was finished with the appropriate furnishings and suits of armor. Its double windows stand out

along with the coats of arms of the Castile and León provinces which decorate the Mudejar friezes and the mural representing the coronation of Isabella, the work of Segovian artist Carlos Muñoz de Pablos.

The Pineapple room takes its name from the sumptuous golden «mocarabes» which are used as pineapples to decorate its coffered ceiling. Its frieze was also restored and it has a magnificent Flemish tapestry and a huge decorated Spanish cabinet.

The Royal Dormitory houses together with several tapestries, an excellent copy of «The Pietá» by Van Weyden, the original of which is kept in Madrid's Prado Museum. The Room of the Kings shows us a frieze with a continuous gallery on which the Spanish Kings and Queens from Don Pelayo to Juana la Loca are all carved out. In the Sala del Cordón (Rope Room), our attention is drawn to an ivory chest. The Queen's

Chamber contains a copy of the «Virgen of the Catholic Monarchs» which is also in the Prado Museum and in the Chapel, the altarpiece is attributed to Portillo. There is also an «Adoration» by Carducho. Behind the very beautiful Patio of the Clock we reach the rooms in which the Museum of Arms has been installed containing some very interesting pieces belonging to the 15th to 18th centuries, including some artillery pieces, bombards, mortars and, of course, a great deal of armor and crossbows. The museum gives us a very complete sampling of the offensive and defensive armament of the epoch.

Finally, in order to culminate our visit to one of the three great symbols of Segovia, the Alcázar, the slender spire of the Torre del Homenaje (the keep), always alert and on guard in the Castilian skies, dressed in fresh slate. From the top we can obtain a splendid view of some of the most beautiful scenery to be seen in this city.

Along this route, in addition to what we have already mentioned, every other detail, no matter how minimal it may seem —the corner of a coffered ceiling, the termination of a seat of honor, the framed design of a window— is certainly worthy of our attention: Everything is art and everything is history.

Eugenio Noel will help us conclude our visit with his phrase: «The arête is cut like the ship's prow, the rock raises the Castle to an unlikely height with wild majesty».

The Alcázar castle. An aerial view.

The Alcázar. The Galley Room.
The Alcázar. The Patio of Arms.
Stained-glass windows.

 The Throne room.
↑ An aerial view.
→ The Alcázar.
□→ The «bow» of the Alcázar.

Churches and monasteries

If the Aqueduct, the Cathedral and the Alcázar mark the substantial triangle of Segovia, its intimate reality, its spiritual essence, could be found in its churches and monasteries, just as the echo of its unforgettable, historical yesterday can only be found in its noble mansions.

We should walk through the city on a random route, following our spontaneous instincts, rather than a city map or a guide book and we should not let ourselves be influenced in the least by the points of the compass. Let us consider the fact that a dozen of its thirty Romanesque churches from the 11th to the 13th centuries continue to function. Two other churches have been partially reformed and they guard some of their original elements, and four more have been transformed today in order to house diverse artistic-cultural missions.

The oldest church is San Juan de los Caballeros, with one of the most beautiful pórticos not only of the city but of all Spanish Romanesque architecture. Historian Diego de Colmenares, whom we have already mentioned, was its parish priest and he was buried in the apse to the side of the Gospel. At the beginning of our century, ceramic artist Daniel Zuloaga purchased the temple, which he restored in order to install his home and workshop. The church today houses the museum dedicated to this illustrious artist and it contains many ceramic pieces of great value and several paintings by his nephew painter Ignacio Zuloaga.

On the location of a previous church, in the quarter which bears its name, the ancient Morería (Moorish quarter), the Church of San Millán stands. In «perennial decline», according to the poetic and amorous voice of Jaime Delgado, «where the Eastern light revives/its psalm day by day». San Millán has been compared on occasions with the Cathedral of Jaca. Three naves, four apses and two atriums define its profile. We should contemplate the capitals of the atrium and on the inside, the final arcade as an altarpiece, the stained glass windows of Muñoz de Pablos· and the processional carvings of Aniceto Marinas, who was baptised there.

In the Plaza de las Sirenas (Mermaid Square) —we should really call it the Square of the Sphinxes— which is named thusly because of its two statues, we can admire the Church of San Martín, with a very beautiful atrium which surrounds three of the sides of the

⬆ The Convent of Santa Cruz (The Santo Domingo Cave).

↑   The Apse and Tower of the San Quirce church.

⬅☐   The Santa Cruz Convent.

⬅➡   San Lorenzo. The arcade of the Cloister. The capital.

temple. On the outside, a 12th century marble bas-relief bears the image of St. Martín. The inside of the church was reformed together with the central apse. The main altar is Solomonic in style, dating back to the second half of the 17th century, with an original work by Segovian artist José Vallejo Vivanco. Among the other pieces of value, we should make note of a «Recumbent Christ» with the apocryphal signature of Gregorio Fernández and a «St. John the Baptist» attributed to Pedro de Bolduque.

It would be practically impossible to try to give a complete roster of Segovia's churches. But if we were to ask out-of-town visitors and even those who live in the city, many would certainly say that San Martín and San Millán are worthy of the most admiration.

In passing, we can also admire, in the San Martín church, the beautiful lateral apse which conserves its original lines. Also its brick tower, centered around its church, with three bodies, and its interior chapels which despite the indispensable reforms carried out over the years, still conserve all of their tranquil beauty.

The Church of San Millán is

Mozarabic in its first part but it was subsequently reconstructed in the 12th century, during the reign of Alfonso I of Aragón. We must stop before its three doorways and under its ribbed vault; opposite the Gothic Crucifix of its presbytery and before the 13th century carving of the «Immaculate Conception»; and finally, we should have a look at the remains of its Mudejar coffered

ceiling made from five hundred year-old wood.

On the site of a previous church, the nave of the Trinity stands. It contains an interesting altarpiece with paintings done at the beginning of the 16th century by Segovian artists Andrés López and Antón de Vega, a panel of the «Holy Face» by Ambrosius Benson, and a very beautiful 17th century polychrome «Immaculate Conception». In 1513. Pedro del Campo and Francisca de la Trinidad had a chapel constructed for their burial, set beside the Gospel. It is necessary to stop before the stained glass windows of «Christ resurrected» and «The Mass of St. Gregory», which are among the oldest in the city. Another more beautiful panel is conserved. It is

⬆ The Cathedral.
⬅▢ San Esteban. The arcade of the Cloister.
⬅ San Martín.

↑ The San Millán Church.
←☐ San Millán. The facade.
← San Lorenzo. The arcade of the Cloister.

from the Florentine school and represents «The Virgin with the Child and St. John». There is also a fine 16th century carving of St. Bartholomew.

San Esteban is especially noted for its magnificent tower fifty-three meters high, «Queen of the Byzantine towers». Along with the tower, only the atrium is conserved from the original construction. As is usual in this city, there is a beautiful pórtico with very lovely capitals. The church has a 13th century Gothic Calvary in polychrome wood. The right arm of the Christ is not nailed down, according to a legend which is similar to the famous tradition of Toledo's Cristo de la Vega shrine. Several of the paintings, apparently belonging to the Italian school, are of considerable importance and among them are two hanging on the walls —«The Baptism of Christ» and «The Preaching of the Baptist», and two found in the Presbytery, «The Virgen with the Child» and «The Annunciation of the Virgin», attributed to Giovanni Odazzi.

The Church of San Lorenzo presides the suburban quarter of the same name. This church has one single, covered nave and three

apses and it was erected on the site of an old Mozarabic structure. Its Gothic brick tower is the only one in the city.

And in order to avoid making our visit as lengthy as it would deserve, we should limit ourselves to admiring the Romanesque paintings of San Justo and its slender calcareous tower; the high-relief and the «Savior» of Gregorio Fernández, in San Andrés; the triptych of the «Adoration of the Kings», attributed to Pieter Coecke van Aeist, in the Church of El Salvador, the mural paintings of San Clemente; the mermaid which shapes one of the capitals of San Quirce —headquarters today for Segovia's Academy of History and Art—; the tomb of Rodrigo Ibáñez in an apse of San Nicolás; the painting of St. Barbara, attributed to a follower of Rubens, Pieter van Avont, in the Gothic temple of San Miguel; and the Romanesque remains of «The Cloister» or the old «Canons», an area which enjoyed the privilege of being able to grant asylum.

Segovia's wealth of churches and monasteries is truly astonishing. And if the route we have outlined for the churches is followed and admired by our readers, the same will be the case for the monasteries. And remember that we are not trying

to give exhaustive information on any of the subjects we have mentioned, but far from it. We only hope to whet the curiosity of the visitor and stimulate his thirst for knowledge, as well as his desire to make his own discoveries —the figures of a capital, the astonishing stability of a ribbed vault, the stony embrace of an apse, a painting half-hidden behind a majestic column, the slender grace of a polychrome carving— discoveries which, in the end, will be of greater interest to him and will represent an experience to cherish forever.

But let us visit, ever so briefly, the treasured route of Segovia's monasteries and convents. Without following any exact chronology, we can begin our route with the Convent of Santo Domingo, the first to be founded by Santo Domingo de Guzmán in Spain. Its origins are rooted in the year 1217 and this surprises us, especially in view of its exceptional Gothic doorway with Hispanic-Flemish influences, which opens the way to this very characteristic church. The tympanum contains statues of the Catholic Monarchs in prayer and they were in fact paid for by the Queen herself. At the upper part is a very elaborate and unusual Calvary set between two Dominicans and on either side, the royal coats of arms. Between the Monarchs is a representation of the Pietá. The temple has one single nave, which has a running chain in endless succession, of the afore-mentioned coats of arms, the royal initials and the historical motto of «Tanto monta, monta tanto» (attributing equal

The Church of San Juan de los Caballeros.
San Millán. The arcade of the Cloister.

↑ The Church of San Esteban.
← ☐ The Church of the Trinity.
← San Andrés. The tower.

35

↑↑ The Monastery of El Parral. The Cloister.
↑ The Church of San Martín.
→ The Monastery of El Parral. The altar-piece.
□→ The Monastery of El Parral. A scenic view.

importance to King Ferdinand and Queen Isabella... and vice versa). It is necessary to contemplate the penitential cave of Santo Domingo and in the Sacristy, the panel of «The Crucified Christ», by Pedro Berruguete.

A synagogue in the 13th century, the Convent of Corpus Christi was converted into a Christian church two centuries later and then it was destroyed at the end of the 19th century. Today, it is occupied by nuns of the St. Clare Order. It has two very interesting altarpieces and its beautiful legend concerning the miraculous song of the Sacred Host was reflected in a painting by Vicente Cutanda (1902) which can be seen at the entrance. In accordance with the legend, a Jewish doctor bought the Sacred Host from a sextan and he tried, with the help of some friends, to cook it in a large pot of water. But as he was about to drop the wafer into the pot, if flew away and at the same time, the Synagogue collapsed.

During the middle of the 15th century, in 1455, Enrique IV founded San Antonio el Real, which was first used as a country palace. He soon turned it over to the Franciscan

monks, who left it at the end of the same century in order to join the Monastery of San Francisco, then the Artillery Academy. The Monastery of San Francisco el Real has a Flemish, polychrome Calvary, which is the only one of its kind in Spain and it integrates the relief of the Crucifixion in the foreground and the «Descent from the Cross» in the background. The entire work is surrounded by scenes from the Passion which have been practically reduced to miniature. The reliquary image of San Antonio de Padua, in silver enamelling, stands out from among the many works of art of all kinds which are kept in the museum installed there, as well as in the monastic rooms.

From the old building of San Francisco, already mentioned, two bodies of the Cloister are conserved, which are of Hispanic-Flemish Gothic style and they are truly outstanding in the City. Special attention should be drawn to the openwork of its parapets and the flight of the tribulated arches found in the upper body.

In 1574, Santa Teresa de Jesús founded the Convent of Discalced Carmelites, located opposite the Church of San Andrés. It seems that Luis Salvador Carmona was the author of «St. Joseph with the Child» which presides the main altarpiece.

According to the traditional line of the Company of Jesus, the Seminary, an old Convent of the same Company, responds to lines set forth by one of the brothers, Andrés Ruiz. The work was carried out by Diego de Matienzo and, upon his death, by his son-in-law, Diego de Sisniega. Pedro de Brizuela and Francisco Gutiérrez de la Cotera also took part in its construction, along with Juan de Mugaguren, the author of the magnificent Baroque patio of three bodies. In the very large church, its main altar stands out, with paintings by Diego Díez Ferreras. The altar was the work of José Vallejo Vivanco, with a gigantic tabernacle, which is also Baroque and which is lined with two enormous wreathed columns on either side.

And on the outside of town is the Sanctuary of La Fuencisla and the Convent of Discalced Carmelites, founded by San Juan de la Cruz, and which would later be the place for his burial. It was built at the end of the second decade of the 17th century and has a single nave and lateral chapels, all of which are presented in an ambience full of simplicity and withdrawal. Aside from some valuable paintings, almost all our attention should be devoted to the Mausoleum of the Saint, in marble and bronze, found in the chapel immediately beside the Gospel.

And finally, in order to complete this journey to the different

⬉ The Arch of the Fuencisla Sanctuary.
⬅ The Fuencisla Sanctuary.

38

The Convent of San Juan de la Cruz.

The Tomb of San Juan de la Cruz.

San Millán.

monasteries, we should follow the Eresma Valley, in order to visit the Monastery of El Parral.

The Segovia proverb says that «From the orchards of the Parral, an earthly paradise» and no-one can present any arguments to the contrary. Of Mudejar influence, with notable echoes of the Monastery of Guadalupe, the Parral complex is grandiose and it allows us to contemplate from afar and enjoy its profiles as we draw closer to it. Enrique IV and the Marquis of Villena, Juan Pacheco, gave emphasis to the origin of the area, where the King established the Spanish Order of the Hieronymites.

Deserted and abandoned during approximately one century, the Monastery suffered a great deal of damage and losses, including the choir stalls, which ended up in the Archaeological Museum and in the Church of San Francisco el Grande, in Madrid.

On the inside, of special interest is the gigantic altarpiece of the main chapel. It is a triple piece in stone and gilded wood which presides the enormous, empty Gothic nave. Juan Cuas, Juan de Ruesga, Sebastián de Almonacid, Juan Rodríguez and Diego de Urbina were some of the artists who took part in the over-all construction of the Monastery, in

which we should contemplate as well the doorway of the Sacristy and the carved alabaster tomb of the Marquis and Marchioness of Villena.

We should skirt the city of Segovia. We can tour its outskirts and first, of course, we should cover the immediate area. We are obliged to begin with the Sanctuary of La Fuencisla, the Patroness and mediator for Segovia. Near the confluence of the Eresma and Clamores rivers, exactly under the impressive mass of the so-called «Grajeras mountains», at the foot of a great boulevard surrounded by crystal clear springs, we come to a favorite spot for pilgrimages, weddings and all kinds of family and romantic events.

In the basic Segovian verse of Jaime Delgado, the Virgin «looks and blesses the alliance» of both water sources, as a unitary symbol of its dear, historical missión. And once more, the legend —collected by the Wise King, Alfonso, in his «Cantigas» (Ballads)— fuses with the reality and here, it is joined by a miracle. It seems that the imagen of the Saint was hidden during the Arab domination in the Church of San Gil, a parish church which has since disappeared. When the image was recovered, a popular legend tells us of a young Jewish girl who

was unjustly condemned for adultery to be hurled off of a cliff to her death. But as the girl was about to be thrown into the Eresma, from the Peñas Grajeras, she prayed to the Patron Saint and said: «Virgin of the Christians, save me!». Our Lady carried the girl through the air and deposited her gently on the ground. The Jewess converted to Christianity and changed her name from Esther to María. The story has since been called the Tale of «María del Salto» (Mary of the Precipice) which we mentioned several chapters back when we spoke of her burial.

The primitive Sanctuary of the 13th century was replaced by the present one somewhere between the 16th and 17th centuries. Inside the grille work of the presbytery stands out in a special manner, together with the iron pulpit donated by Juan de Monreal and the magnificent altarpiece by Pedro de la Torre and José de Rates, made up of seven canvases, two of which are by Francisco Camilo and others are by Cristóbal Pérez de Teruel. The altar is completed with an «Assumption of the Virgin», by Ribera.

The Baroque Sacristy is indeed beautiful and along the boulevard, the 18th century Arch of La Fuencisla, with the coat of arms of the city and the figures of the Virgin and María del Salto. In the treasury room of the Virgin, we find jewels and clothes and the crown offered by popular collection for her canonical coronation in 1916.

◥ Vera Cruz. The central nave.
◩ Vera Cruz. The facade.

⬆ The Vera Cruz church.
⬅▢ Vera Cruz. The interior.
⬅ Vera Cruz. The altar-piece.

41

On the shores of the river, in the Casa de la Moneda (The Mint), built by Felipe II, with plans possibly drawn up by Herrera, the Monarch coined the most perfect money of the epoch.

Abandoned and sold, to be used as a flour factory, the building caught fire and its structure has since been modified.

The traces of San Juan de la Cruz are indelible in this land and his tomb was especially visited by Pope John Paul II during his visit to Spain for the Pope had written his doctorate on the Saint's work. In the valley of the Eresma river, where the Convent of the Trinitarios de Santa María de Rocamador once stood, San Juan founded, with the help of Ana de Peñalosa, the Convent of the Discalced Carmelites. He was prior of the Convent from 1588 until the beginning of 1591. A few months later he died in Ubeda and a couple of years later he was buried in the Convent which he had founded.

To the north of the City, beyond the Eresma, beside the Zamarramala highway, there is a very unusual church, the most

unique of Segovia's Romanesque churches: the Church of Vera Cruz or of the Knights of Templar. It was constructed in 1203 by the Order of the Templars and when this order was dissolved, the church was turned over to the Order of Malta, until the 17th century. The Provincial Commission of Monuments was responsible for preventing the destruction of the church in 1845.

When the visitor faces the Church of the Vera Cruz, he cannot help but feel himself transported to another time, another epoch. It is like a trip back in time —its construction is dated at the end of the Romanesque period, in the year 1208 to be exact— in search of a historical past, which is frequently so vague that we cannot distinguish the legend from the reality, the real people from the mythical ones. This obscure situation which makes it so difficult to specify any exact information has spread to a broad fan of other structures which could serve as mirrors for reflecting the newer work. This offering extends from the Church of Eulate, in

Navarre, to the Holy Sepulcher, itself, in Jerusalem, including, obviously, all of the other temples which belonged to the different military orders. Its slender tower greets us from the distance but when we come closer, even our least imaginative minds cannot help but fly back in time, with a desire to unearth the one thousand mysteries which are rooted in the hundred year-old walls.

A shrine dedicated to the Santa Cruz (Holy Cross) and donated by Honorio III in 1226, appears to have given origin to its name. In 1951, it returned to the Order of Malta which restored it and valuable paintings are found on its walls. To the original twelve-sided polygonal design, three apses and a tower were added. A stone tablet is found in the central building where the knights must have carried out the vigil of their arms. There is also a Gothic-Renaissance altarpiece dated in 1516 and the «Lignum Crucis» was kept in a niche in the chapel of the tower until it was removed to the parish church of Zamarramala, where it can be admired today.

We will leave the outskirts of the city at this point in order to get to know other parts of the province wich deserve our attention and a cordial leisurely visit.

↘ The El Parral Monastery. The facade.
↰ San Juan de los Caballeros. The arcade.

⬆ The El Parral Monastery.

⬅⬜ El Parral. Tomb of Juan Pacheco.

⬅ El Parral. Tomb of Beatriz Pacheco.

⊢□ La Granja. The Palace and gardens.
↑↑↑ La Granja. Neptune fountain.
↑↑ La Granja. Gardens.
↑ An aerial view of the La Granja Palace.
⊢ A part of the fountain. La Granja.

La Granja

The Royal Palace of San Ildefonso served as the hunting grounds for the Monarchs of Castile. Enrique IV had a shrine built there in order to satisfy his religious obligations and he offered it to Saint Ildefonso. The Catholic Monarchs donated the sanctuary to the Hieronymite Order of the Monastery of El Parral and the monks, in turn, built a farm nearby for rest, relaxation and convalescence.

The idea of building a palace here belonged to Felipe V who also wanted to surround the palace with gardens which would rival those of the French Palace of Versalles. He intended La Granja (The Farm) to be used as a summer residence for the Royal Court. Several fires made restoration work necessary but the whole which can be visited today is indeed exceptional.

Just eleven kilometers from Segovia, the facade of this Palace measures 155 meters in length and 13 meters in height. The side sections of the Palace are 45 meters long and they were built at a later date. In the rear, the Collegiate Church, in the shape of a Latin cross, conserves the Pantheon where the remains of Felipe V and Isabel de Farnesio rest.

It would be almost impossible to summarize even with a minimal sketch, all of the artistic treasures contained here. We are talking only about the 145 hectares which the Palace and the surrounding gardens occupy and the ten thousand trees of the most varied species which make up its forest.

Among the world famous fountains, we can mention «The Fame» (whose jet sends water forty-seven meters into the air), «Neptune», «Andromeda», «Apollo», «Amphitrite», «The three graces», «Of the Dragons», «Of the Frogs», «Diana's bath», «The Basket» and a long etcetera which make up a total of 140 incomparably artistic fountains.

Inside of the Palace is an exceptional collection of tapestries from Brussels and from Madrid's Royal Factory of Santa Barbara, which is considered to be possibly the top factory in all Europe. Paintings by Lucas Jordán, Miguel Angel Houasse, Constanzi, Trevisani, Rosa de Tivoli, Gian Paolo Panini, Louis Michel Van Loo... Frescos by Bartolomé Rusca; 18th century clocks; Imperial crystal and bronze chandeliers; in all, a unique collection which demands a careful, thorough visit from the traveller.

The marvelous gardens represent the sucessive work of René Carlier and Esteban Boutelou, and they are decidedly geometric in their design. And their creative imagination was seasoned with a broad sculptural sampling which accompanies the prodigious chain of its fountains, with statues in marble and lead painted with a very characteristic green color, by the Dumandré brothers, Fremin, Bouseau, Pisúe and Thierri.

↘ La Granja.
↑ Neptune fountain.
→ The facade of the La Granja Palace.

The Province

The first stop, ten kilometers from Segovia and twelve from San Ildefonso, is necessarily the Palace of Riofrío, a source of infinite surprise to anyone who travels along this route without any previous knowledge of its existence. Surrounded by 700 hectares of oak wood, where big game lives and multiplies, Riofrío was the frequent site for royal hunts in the times of Alfonso XII and Alfonso XIII. Isabel de Farnesio pressed for the construction of the Palace which was finalized by Carlos III.

A Neo-classical square building, with a very valuable and unusual collection of artwork, the **Riofrío** Palace is the ideal setting for today's Hunting Museum. Its central patio is very attractive and the Main or Honor Staircase is magnificent and one of the most grandiose in our country. Construction was begun in 1752 according to plans drawn up by Italian architect Virgilio Rabaglio.

Its pink ornamental decorations and its green coffered balconies treasure some very artistic pieces of the most varied styles. Thus, the series of one hundred and fifty paintings entitled «The Life of Our Lord Jesus Christ», attributed to the Florentine artist Camilo Segrestani. There are also paintings by Houasse, Domenico María Sani, Giacomo Nani..., one attributed to Ribera and others by Ricardo Madrazo, José Calofre and Ramón Casas.

Furniture, lamps, clocks and tapestries complete the collection which has been embellished since 1970 with the afore-mentioned Museum, which shows among other pieces of great value, the «Cuerna del venado» (The Deer's Antlers), by Velázquez, tapestry designs on cardboard by Maella and Goya, and other examples of similar importance.

But the province is big and of multiple interest no matter what the direction chosen for our cultural or touristic excursions. We can mention, for example, the Palace House of Contreras and the 16th century City Hall building in **Ayllón;** the beautiful altarpiece with twenty-two paintings by artists Baltasar Grande and Diego Rosales, disciples of Ambrosio Benson, found in the early 16th century Church of **Carbonero el Mayor;** in the church of San Eutropio, in the **El Espinar** parish, a splendid altarpiece by Francisco Giralte, Juan Manzano and Vicente Espinosa, which includes paintings by Alonso Sánchez Coello; or the parish church of Santa María la Mayor, in **Fuentepelayo,** with sculptures by Pedro Bolduque and beautiful gold and silver work, including a Gothic monstrance and the Plateresque processional cross.

In **Martín Muñoz de las Posadas,** beside the Palace of Cardinal Diego de Espinosa, we can admire in the late Gothic parish church, the tomb of the General Inquisitor and Bishop of Sigüenza,

⊥ Sepúlveda. An aerial view.

↑ The Riofrío Palace. An aerial view.
⬅☐ Riofrío. The outskirts.
➡ The El Salvador Church of Sepúlveda.

Cardinal Diego de Espinosa, who was born in this town. The alabaster tomb was the work of Pompeyo Leoni. There is also a polychrome San Marcos by Manuel Pereira and a possible Goya in the Sacristy, representing the Crucifixion, though its final authenticity seems difficult to prove.

Riaza is a summer vacation spot, with a Plaza Mayor worthy of mention because of its typical appearance and because it is one of the best in the province and in the rest of the country, for that matter. On the outskirts of the town stands the ancient Sanctuary of Our Lady of Hontanares.

In **Santa María la Real de Nieva,** its 14th century Gothic church has an interesting Plateresque altarpiece, a sculpture attributed to Alonso Berruguete or to his workshop and an exceptional processional cloister.

`Sotosalbos offers us its magnificent Romanesque church with its strong, square tower and in its vicinity, the ruins of the 13th century Cistercian monastery dedicated to Santa María de la Sierra, Patroness of the town.

Trescasas, just eight kilometers from the capital, with seven canvases making up the altarpiece of its parish church; a «Purísima» (Immaculate Conception) by Maella and the remaining six works by Goya's brother-in-law, Ramón Bayeu. And Villacastín, with its Herrerian church attributed to the architect of Segovia's Cathedral, Rodrigo Gil de Hontañón.

We can, for example, skirt the province to the north and stop in **Coca,** with its long and busy history. Here we can admire the granite boars sculpted by the Celts or the tomb of the master of the city, the Fonseca family, in the Gothic church of Santa María. A little farther on

and we come to **Cuéllar,** with its inevitable view of the Convent of San Franciso, which was restored by Beltrán de la Cueva. The tower House cannot be overlooked nor the Romanesque apses of its churches of San Andrés, San Esteban and San Martín.

If we cross **Fuentesaúco,** we come to what was once the residence of Alfonso VIII on some occasions, **Fuentidueña.** The Romanesque apse of the Church of San Martín which is in ruins today has ended up in the Museum of New York no less. And if we continue in a direction which we will also follow for the Castle route, we will come to **Sepúlveda,** the ancient Septempública, the town of the seven gateways, with noble mansions such as those of the Moro (Moor), of the Conchas (Shells) —built at the beginning of the 17th century—, of the Count of

Sepúlveda, and of the González family, apart from the churches of San Justo, San Bartolomé and Santiago. Later on, we will make mention of its castle. We could follow many other routes, but we do not propose to offer an exhaustive study of the province and it is now time to turn our attention to the Castle Route.

⊥ Sepúlveda. Church of Our Lady of la Peña.

↑ Sotosalbos. The Church.
←▢ Ayllón. The facade of the Contreras Palace.
← Coca.

↑ ↑ ↑ Coca Castle. The moat.
↑ ↑ Coca Castle. A partial view.
↑ Coca Castle. The entrance.
→ Coca Castle. An aerial view.

The Castle Route

Segovia is a province which is very rich in castles. If we extend the specific area to include its surroundings, we remember the words of the Marquis of Lozoya, that «the number of castles gave name to the prominent region which would be its central nucleus». The author himself has felt that «the sign of the dispersion» was the medieval cause and origin of such a proliferation of fortresses «against the always possible attack of a neighbor».

Apart from the Alcázar, that prow of all Segovia, that proud, historical challenger, the North star and example for generations to come, that castle which was also the first in its lands and the foundation for the rocks which caress and sing more than the waters of the Eresma and Clamores. Many are the itineraries which we can follow in order to get to know the most characteristic of this noble and legendary land.

We can follow just any route because our aim is basically to travel around the province. We can, for example, take the road to Coca and stop at **Santa María la Real de Nieva,** which was founded in the second half of the 19th century. We will visit its Gothic church and of special interest is its Cloister, of transitional Romanesque style and its outstanding altarpiece attributed to Berruguete.

The arrival at **Coca,** the

Celt-Iberian Cauca, the home and cradle in the fourth century of Teodosius the Great, gives us the opportunity to contemplate the unmatched silhouette of its castle, the most perfect example of Mudejar architecture of a military nature. Where the Eresma and Voltoya rivers meet, Archbishop Alonso de Fonseca had the castle built at the beginning of the 15th century. A town of old Castilian flavor, its castle took most of the 15th century to complete and it is made of brick, surrounded by a wide and deep moat. Four hexagonal towers stand at the corners and the battlement keep presides over the exceptional

structure. The Duke of Medina Sidonia was kept prisoner here in 1645 after his unsuccessful attempt to proclaim himself king of Andalusia. Such was the ostentation found in its salons and grand halls that, after a banquet dinner, Alfonso de Fonseca had a series of trays filled with jewels and gems carried among the female guests so that they could choose the baubles which most pleased them. The Castle underwent sacking and suffered serious damage over the years. It was restored by the Ministry of Agriculture in such a way that all of its ancestral grandeur can now be admired from the outside.

We can leave the Eresma, heading for Cega, and scarcely thirty kilometers away, we come to the walled-in city of **Cuéllar,** the second city of the province, the ancient Celt-Iberian Colenda, one of the most outstanding Moorish-Romanesque complexes in Spain. It has four parish churches, those of San Esteban, San Martín,

↑ Cuéllar Castle.
← Cuéllar. Santa María Magdalena Hospital.

⬆ Pedraza Castle.
⬅⬜ Pedraza. Plaza Mayor.
⬅ A partial view of Sepúlveda.

San Andrés and El Salvador, which were the first of their kind, in Romanesque style, with brick construction and surprising apses. At the highest point in the area, Alfonso X had a tower built and a castle was constructed beside it in the 15th century by King Enrique IV's favorite, Beltrán de la Cueva. A fortified moat defended the flanks except for the one which stood guard over the town itself, with its three cylindrical and one square towers at the corners. Succesive reconstructions combined the Gothic style and added Mudejar and Renaissance touches, along with the Arabic arch at the main entrance. The later palace was built in the central patio. Upon the death of her father, the followers of the Beltraneja met in this castle in order to stand up to the followers of Isabella and Ferdinand, who had gathered in the Castle of Coca. The Castle later belonged to the Duque of Alburquerque and Espronceda was held prisoner here.

We can go from the Cega to the Duratón and we will come to **Fuentidueña,** with the remains of a once powerful castle, possessing a long belicose history. Remains are also found from the two Romanesque castles and not far away from the old bridge over the river is the beginning of the stone crossroads which will take us to San Juan de la Penitencia, a Franciscan convent.

If we descend the Duratón another thirty kilometer, we come to **Sepúlveda,** beside the waters of the Castilla, at a height which is dominated by the 11th century Romanesque church of El Salvador

which affords us an impressive view like a natural watchtower over the town. Many homes with coats of arms, vestiges of the ramparts and the old castle on the square and the Romanesque church of the Virgen de la Peña, the Patroness, has made Sepúlveda one of the most delightful places for the traveller to visit.

We can head towards Pedraza, once again in the direction of the Cega, and we leave the Castle of **Castilnovo** on our left, amidst thick forests. It is square in shape, surrounded by barbicans and six towers joined by brief sections of wall and artistic battlements. Everything began with the eighth century Arab fortress until the Aragonese kings built a castle which later belonged to Alvaro de Luna and the Catholic Monarchs, until it reached the hands of the Marquis of Quintanar.

With one single doorway through the ramparts, we come to **Pedraza,** presided over by the Romanesque tower of San Juan. It was perhaps the birthplace of Trajan. The painter Ignacio Zuloaga bought a large fortified tower in the castle in 1928 in order to set up his studio and it is the only part of the structure which is not now in ruins. It is famous for its main square with an arcade and the «Elm of the Town Council».

Very nearby, to the northwest, is **Turégano,** the episcopal and Castilian town, also just thirty kilometers from the capital. It was in fact the bishop Juan Arias Dávila who ordered the construction of the castle in the 15th century, around the Romanesque church of San Miguel, which had been built two

◥ Pedraza. Church tower.
◀ Castilnovo Castle.

↑ Sepúlveda Castle.
←□ Cuéllar. Aristocratic coats of arms.
⇆ Sotosalbos. The Image of the Virgen de la Sierra.

We can continue this itinerary or any other, travel to the North or to the South, follow highways or seek out rivers, or stop off at one of the many towns along our route. It really doesn't matter. Our trip will always be marked by beautiful discoveries. And by the existence of this unparalleled rosary of castles which are in turn accompanied by another parallel caravan of pleasant landscape and samples of extraordinary artwork.

And so the magnificent decoration of the Castle of Castilnovo, which has always been inhabited (this is not frequently the case). It once belonged to the Marquis of Villena and to the Prince of Hohenzollern, until it reached the hands of its present owners. Or the pure line of Gregorio Fernández reflected in the image on the «Immaculate Conception» which we can admire in the parish church of Turégano. Or the royal Baroque balcony of the House of the Count and Countess of Sepúlveda, in the town of the same name. Or the arched entranceway of the town of Pedraza. Or, in Cuéllar, the paintings by Lucas Jordán (San Joaquín, Santa Ana and the Virgin Girl) which are kept on display in the Church of San Miguel in the main square. Or, in Coca, the brick tower and rubble work of the Church of San Nicolás.

centuries before. And there was probably another fortress existing earlier still, in the twelfth century, as evidenced by certain ruins of the ramparts. There was also an important prisoner kept here, Antonio Pérez, who was secretary to King Felipe II. The main square of the town is universally renown and we must also visit the Church of Santiago. The old Patio of Arms of the Castle was covered in its entirety in the times of the afore-mentioned Bishop in order to be able to expand thusly the capacity of the chapel, to that of a church presided over by a slender bell gable. Fernando el Católico stayed in the castle until his coronation in Segovia and Alfonso I el Batallador had a major argument here with his wife, Doña Urraca. And in this town which Fernán González won over from the Moors, Juan II and Alvaro de Luna reached a historical reconciliation.

Everything is history, art, monumentality, beauty. Everything is living stone and the testimony of a glorious past. Everything is the essence of the present, visible at every stop in this unmatched route of Segovian castles.

↘ Pedraza Castle.
← The ramparts of Castilnovo Castle.

↑ Turégano Castle.
←□ Turégano Castle.
← Turégano Castle. The tower.

Craftwork and folklore

Textile and ceramic work are typical products of Segovia's craftwork. The textiles have a very long history and their weavers were already famous in far away lands several centuries before. The regional dress of both the men and the women make up by themselves a faithful testimony of the wealth of the materials and the art and skill of the hand-made work which goes into everything from the female's filigreed head-dress to the male's strong, virile waistcoat.

The ceramic work has seen a lot of its patterns disappear as is the case most everywhere. However we can still find some magnificent pieces used as toys by Otilio Bautista and the surviving models of jugs for wine which are certainly very popular on even a national scale and other recipients which are

shaped like animals.

In regard to the folklore as expressed in Segovia's popular dances, special mention should be paid to the «paloteo», of the dancers who interrupt their rhythmic stepping from time to time in order to clap their small sticks against one another.

Among the typical fiestas and holidays, mention should be made of the Festivity of the Fuencisla, the last Sunday in September; San Frutos, the 25th of October; the Day of Segovia, which is celebrated on the first Sunday of July; the Fiestas Mayores of San Juan and San Pedro from the 24 to the 29th June. And the popular festivities of Cuéllar, Sepúlveda, Pedraza, Turégano, Riaza and Santa María la Real de Nieva, which is also called the

«Festivity of the Soterraña» (Underground).

The festivity of Santa Agueda is celebrated throughout the province but in a very special way in Zamarramala, just three kilometers from the city. Here the women rule, instead of the men, for a period of twenty-four hours. The magnificent dresses worn by the lady mayor and her «constables» are indeed striking and we cannot overlook the pure linen shirts, the velvet vest, the adorned skirt and silver embroidery on the scarlet or blue velvet.

All of this is a very substantial part of Segovian life, a geography which is fully in love with its traditions. Its treasured customs combine with the magnificent wealth of its monumentality and its art, and the natural beauty of its land and its rivers, conserved with a special delight and pampering by their people who are convinced that they will reflect the very essence of their being to the entire world.

And finally, craftwork and folklore give us a last touch of the Segovia soul. We have tried to bring you near to this soul with our excursions and we hope our readers have been able to get to know a little better the many historical, artistic, cultural and human attractions of the province.

Gastronomy in the capital

When we speak of our Gastronomical Map, Segovia holds a privileged place. The same can be said for its wealth of art, its landscape, its ambience and its light. It also offers a simple and delicious cuisine which men and means have created and which remain intact today.

We arrive at the Azoguejo and there, under the two thousand year old stones of the Aqueduct which Rome has bequeathed to us, I offer to all of you my tavern, my hospitality and, of course (I might as well add), my roast sucking pigs: This is the most characteristic dish of Segovia cooking and my pigs enjoy old world fame.

We enter the City and we can see the restaurants of Amado, César and La Criolla. We continue along the Calle Real in the direction of the Plaza Mayor, past the restaurants of Duque, El Bernardino and El Abuelo. The narrowness of the street brings the delicious smell of typical Castilian soup to our nostrils... thick, stewed beans which are grown in La Granja and seasoned with pig feet and ears, fresh trout from the mountain streams, which should be accompanied by crusty bread and wines from the Ribera del Duero.

And we reach the Plaza Mayor, under the arrogance of the Gothic Cathedral: La Taurina, La Oficina,

and José María; a whole array which are complemented by others such as La Cocina de San Millán, the Venta de la Mina...

Roast lamb made in bread ovens is another specialty. Sepúlveda, Pedraza, Sotosalbos, Torrecaballeros, are places where the traveller can find the blazing oven and in all of them, this succulent dish is served.

The veal from Prádena, the sausages and especially the «chorizo» sausage, from Cantimpalos, loin pork, ham slices, fried bacon, with oil, all go into the «Pot». Special mention should be made of the game: wild boar, deer, quail and partridge which complete this chapter.

The famous mushrooms of the Parral Caves, macerated with old wines; the nut cookies, the sweetened egg yolks («yemas») and the Segovia punch, together with the home-made pastries, close this chapter on sweets with great style. Segovia is also endowed with á National Parador which offers privileged views over the City and a visit to the Hostería restaurant in Pedraza can also be enjoyed.

Cándido
Chief Tavern-keeper of Castile

Gastronomy in the province

If we barely begin to investigate the gastronomy of the land and we try some of the delicacies, we will be obliged to agree with Luis Antonio de Vega's favorite, old initiative of converting Segovia into the seat of a gastronomical archdiocese. And it is very difficult to add even a line to what Cándido has just offered us. We will, however, add that his Mesón (tavern) is found in a 15th century building which is included in the Inventory of Artistic Monuments of the City of Segovia and it has been carrying out its mission since the year 1860, with the same family at the helm.

If, at the end of these pages, in the section on useful addresses, you find a list of a good many restaurants in the province, it is only provided for informative purposes, for in this area, you will find praiseworthy quality at unusually reasonable prices in any of the establishments

you choose. For this reason, we will only discuss what is of interest to us now: Food!

The selection of appetizers available to make our wait for the main dish more agreeable is indeed extensive: asparagus, mushrooms, frog legs, river crabs, tripe, kidneys... all of which comes from the region though some of the dishes may be seasonal.

The most memorable dishes, of course, are the roasts, the lamb and sucking pig, which the master Segovia roasters manage to serve to perfection. Forming an honor guard, we can mention the garlic soup with ham and bacon, the beans with chopped pig's ear, cod and onions in «ajo arriero» (garlic sauce), fried lamb with paprika (plus parsely, garlic, vinegar and salt), pickled or cooked trout, Segovia-style or fried, fish stew, also made with lamb, partridge,

Aqueduct-style, with the fine magic touch of adding chopped, fried bacon.

Of course, you have to try, if possible, the wines of the land, and there are many and with a strong, robust flavor. Particularly famous are those from Pedraza de la Sierra.

And at dessert time, you have a very confusing choice: Of course, the Segovia punch («ponche»), together with sweetened egg yolks («yemas»), sponge cake or bread donuts, with «aguardiente» liquor cannot be missed. And the specific traditional treats such as the «soplillos», from Segovia capital, the «pan sobado» which is enjoyed during the festivities in honor of the Patron Saint of Castro de Fuentidueña, the egg cake with which birthdays are celebrated in many towns of the province, the characteristic «bolillos» (bobbins) of Carnival time or the «palo» donuts, with lemon, cinnamon and white wine which are customarily prepared for Easter Sunday.

There are many more things but it is better for you to discover them for yourself as you make your way through our province.

Useful address and telephone numbers

Segovia

Civil Government Headquarters. Plaza del Seminario, 1. Tel. (911) 43 49 11.
Provincial Government Headquarters. San Agustín, 13. Tel. 43 64 11.
City Hall. Franco, 1. Tel. 43 36 11.
Tourism Delegation. San Facundo, 1. Tel. 43 27 11.
Traffic Headquarters. Tel. 43 34 61.
Fire Department. Tel. 42 22 22.
RENFE (Spanish Railway) Information. Tel. 42 07 74.
Hospital SOE. Tel. 43 63 63.
Teleben (Telegrams). Tel. 22 20 00.
Emergency Medical Attention. Tel. 43 21 61.
Municipal Police Department. Tel. 43 12 12.
Police. Tel. 091.
City Information. Tel. 003.
The «El Adelantado de Segovia» newspaper. San Agustín, 7. Tel. 43 72 61.
Radio Segovia, SER, OM and FM. San Agustín, 3. Tel. 43 62 62.
Antena 3 Radio station FM. Ramón y Cajal, s/n. Tel. 42 88 12.

Hotels

National Parador on the outskirts of town. Tel. 43 07 50.
Acueducto (* * *). Padre Claret, 10. Tel. 42 48 00.
Los Linajes (* * *). Dr. Velasco, 9. Tel. 43 17 12.
Las Sirenas, H (* * *). Juan Bravo, 30. Tel. 43 40 11.
Plaza. Hs (* *). Cronista Lecea, 11. Tel. 43 12 28.
Puerta de Segovia (* * *). Ctra. Soria. Plasencia, s/n. Tel. 43 73 50.

Restaurants

Mesón de Cándido. Azoguejo, 5. Tels. 42 81 02 and 42 81 03. Its has been declared an artistic monument. «Judiones» beans, trouts from their own nursery, crabs... and roast sucking pig, and the chance to see Cándido carve the little pigs with a plate, dressed in his official costume of «Chief Tavern-keeper of Castile».
Casa Amado. Fernández-Lareda, 9. Tel. 43 20 77. Frogs legs in spring and summer, fried hake, delicious bread. This restaurant is a favorite among the Segovians.
La Cocina de San Millán. San Millán, 3. Tel. 43 62 26. Stuffed peppers and chicken salad.
Mesón de Duque. Cervantes, 12. Tel. 43 05 37. Cream of crab soup, «judiones» beans, veal, stuffed partridge, Segovian style. It is the oldest in the city.

Automobiles

Citroën-Peugeot. Guadarrama, 15. Tel. 42 14 05.
Ford. Carretera Madrid. Tel. 42 14 81.
Renault. Peñalara, 2. Tel. 42 26 81.
Seat-Fiat. Carretera de Madrid. Tel. 42 24 74.
Talbot. Avda. de San Rafael, 42. Tel. 42 16 26.

Banks

Bilbao. Azoguejo, 9.
Central. Fernández-Ladreda, 15.
España. Ildefonso Rodríguez, 1.
Español de Crédito. Cervantes, 27.
Hispano Americano. Fernández-Ladreda, 4.
Santander. Fernández-Ladreda, 9.
Caja de Ahorros. Fernández-Ladreda, 2.

IN THE PROVINCE

Cuéllar:

Mesón de San Francisco. San Franciso, 25. Tel. 14 00 09. Rooms. Hs (* *). Sensational lamb. «Suspiros de Monja» (A nun's sighs) dessert.

La Granja:

La Chimenea. Pl. del Molino, 5. Tel. 47 12 62. Specializing in French cooking.
El Pajarón. Carretera de Torrecaballeros, s/n. Tel. 47 09 39. Special trout and cream desserts.
Hotel «El Europeo». España, 9. Tel. 47 03 69.

Valsaín:

La Hilaria. Carretera N-601, km. 74. Tel. 47 02 92.
El Torreón. Carretera Madrid-La Granja. Tel. 47 09 04. Garlic soup and fine wines.

Riofrío:

Riofrío, beside the Palace of the same name. Tel. 48 00 61. Trout and punch pie.

Pedraza:

National Hostería «Pintor Zuloaga». Matadero, 1. Tel. 15, located in the so-called «Inquisition House». «Caldereta» stew; a fine still life by Máximo Manrique. Procuradores, 6. Tel. 8. Castilian soup and wines from Duero.

Riaza:

«La Trucha». H (* *). Doctor Tapia. Tel. 71. A fine restaurant.
La Taurina. Pl. Generalísimo. Tel. 73. Wines from Aranda.

Hostal Casaquemada. HR (*). Tel. 35. An omelette named after the establishment.

Sepúlveda:

Casa Paulino. Calvo Sotelo, 2. Tel. 54 00 16. Meat, fish and excellent wines.
Hijos de Zute el Mayor. José Antonio, 2. Tel. 54 30 25. Only roast lamb, but what lamb! Also salad and goat cheese served with quince jelly.

Torrecaballeros:

La Posada de Javier. Carretera de Soria. Tel. 41. Stew and loin pork with mustard.
Horno de la Aldehuela. Carretera de Soria. Tel. 44. all home-made dishes.

Sotosalbos:

Las Casillas. Tel. 450 29 59. Castilian soup and «chorizo» sausage stew. Manrique. Carretera de Soria. Tel. 17 32 00. Trout, roast pig.

San Rafael:

Lucia. H (*). Carretera de La Coruña, km. 62. Tel. 17 10 02.

Villacastín:

In reality, the entire province is one magnificent roasting oven and in all of the restaurants mentioned, along with the others which mark the one hundred roads and byways, the roast pig and the roast lamb are the unquestionable and undisputed emperors of the cuisine, thanks to their incomparable excellence. For this reason, we will not try to make specific mention of the restaurants for we would have to include each and every one of the «mesones» and taverns in the province. We did not hope to offer an exhaustive list but we would like to single out in **Segovia**, the following: El Bernardino, La Criolla, Galicia, Garrido, Lago, Mesón-cito, La Oficina, El Racimo de Oro, El Pingüino, Casa Basilio, Solaire, El Abuelo. La Taurina, Casa Muñoz, Las Palmeras, El Porvenir, Correos, Postigo, Orensano, Quintanar...
In **Ayllón**, Pemar; in **Boceguillas**, El Pinar; en **Cantalejo**, Casa Marino; in **Cuéllar**, Curro and Florida; in **El Espinar**, La Terraza, El Rolar and Avenida; in **La Lastrilla**, La Venta Mina; in **Martín Muñoz de las Posadas**, Los Rosales; in **Prádena**, Las Tres BBB; in **San Ildefonso**, Madrid, La Terraza, Los Claveles, Maribén, Miami, Segovia, Roma...
It is simply one of the most complete gastronomical maps of all Spain. Hearty appetite and we hope to be seeing you soon!